TRUE TALES
OF THE
FOUR WINDS
Volume 01

David J. Hooton
(Spirit Walker)

ISBN – 13 978-1484886700
ISBN – 10 1484886704

The
FOUR WINDS
Free Trappers
of
Cache Valley, Utah

TWO OWLS

These stories are based on real events and experiences of the Four Winds Free Trappers, and their friends. However, due to the passage of time, a forgetful mind, and for the enjoyment of the reader, some portions of these tales may be slightly embellished.

TRUE TALES
OF THE
FOUR WINDS

The River

The winter frost dwindled to a mild nip in the early morning air, and the afternoon sun could once again leave it's reddened kiss upon one's cheek. This day became different than any other day. On this day, Two Owls became a brother to the deer.

As the morning sun cast its glow on the rock slope to the west, it gave a spectacular show of small, glimmering rainbows within the melting snow. Hundreds, if not thousands, of tiny streams trickled down granite masses in an attempt to join the rapid flow of a springtime river.

"Did you sleep well?" Asked Two Owls as he knelt down next to the fire to pull a black kettle from the flames.

"I did, thanks," replied Spirit Walker. "How about you?"

"Much warmer than nights past." Steam rose from his cup as he poured black sludge from the kettle. "It looks like it will be a nice day."

"I hope so," replied Spirit Walker, admiring the moment.

Skunk Britches stepped out of his lodge with a bucket in one hand, and a shirt in the other. He shivered as he draped the long hunter shirt over his medicine pole ties, and poured water over his head. He shook for a moment, and pushed his arms into the sleeves of the shirt.

"I feel much better now," he said, rolling a stump around to sit by the fire.

Two Owls remained crouched by the fire and pulled a wooden pipe from his side pouch. While filling it with tobacco, he gave the slight head nod hello to Sly Fox, who had just sat next to Spirit Walker.

Bright blue eyes stared out from beneath locks of thick, black hair as he pulled a stick from the fire, placed the burning end near his pipe, and puffed a couple times. Smoke curled around his face as he puffed a few more times, giving the illusion of Black Beard after canon fire. "Where's your brothers?" He asked, savoring the taste of Cavendish.

"Lone Wolf went for a walk upstream," answered Sly Fox as he poured himself a second cup of coffee. "Badger is still eating his breakfast in the lodge."

"They can catch up later. Let's get some work done before it gets to hot, and I need a nap?"

"I'm ready," replied Spirit Walker, placing his empty cup near the fire ring.

"I hope they hurry." Two Owls emptied the ash from his pipe and placed it back in it's pouch. "We need all the help we can get." He stood and moved toward the river.

"If we were trapping instead of lumber jacking," said Sly Fox, stepping over a fallen tree. "Our pelts wouldn't be worth a thing. They're already losing their winter coats."

"What did you say?" Skunk Britches asked. "I can't hear a thing being this close to the loud river." He quickly moved closer to Sly Fox.

"I said the pelts wouldn't be worth a thing."

Two Owls stopped and stared at an approaching figure.

A tall, slender man, wearing a yellow head rag ducked through the trees and joined them at the waters edge. It was Lone Wolf.

"There are two more dams to break down about a hundred yards ahead," he gestured toward a bend in the river. "There are a few deer drinking up there too."

"Are the dams anything like this one?" Asked Sly Fox as he tossed a few stones into the water.

"No, this one is the largest."

They all stood still for a moment at the edge of the dam, pondering the method of removal. Water splashed into the air as it hit the fallen trees, and chewed it's way through the banks on each side of the dam.

"If we want to stay dry in camp, we need to pull these trees out," said Two Owls, carefully stepping into the water and taking hold of an overhanging branch. "Be careful, this water could kill us in an instant." He changed his footing and took another step into the raging water.

Hearts raced with fear as the thought of Two Owls being swept away clawed at everyone's mind.

"I'll move this mess to the bank and the rest of you pull them out," yelled Two Owls, struggling with the smaller branches, and the current.

Skunk Britches, Sly Fox, and Lone Wolf hesitantly joined Two Owls in the waist deep, rushing water, and Badger, Running moon, and Morning Star joined Spirit Walker in pulling the mess into the tall grass.

Branch after branch, and tree after tree, we, as a family, pulled the dam apart. Water rushed down the river with greater force, and more force meant quicker erosion. They watched as dirt ripped from the banks, and debris washed away in the growing current. One down, two to go.

One, by one, the drenched men crawled onto the bank and let the water flow from their clothes. Then, one to another, they complained about the freezing, fast moving water.

"I need to stand by the fire," said Lone Wolf, removing his shirt to ring it out. "My legs are numb."

"Mine are numb as well," replied Skunk Britches, who was already several steps away.

Sly Fox quickly split a few logs and tossed them toward Two Owls, who made sure the fire grew large, and hot. Flames quickly engulfed the dry wood, sending waves of heat and sparks in all directions.

"What happened to your arm?" Asked Morning Star, grabbing hold of Lone Wolf's elbow to reveal a stream of blood.

"I'm not sure. I was hit by many things rushing down the river." He pulled the yellow cloth from his head and tied it around his wound. "A branch must have hit me harder than I thought."

"I told you that the river was dangerous," Said Two Owls, turning to admire their work. He then dropped the wood he was holding and ran toward the river.

Everyone watched in amazement as a young

doe sprang from the water, lost her balance, and disappeared beneath the raging current just as Two Owls jumped into the river. He too vanished beneath the rapids.

"Oh my God," screamed Spirit Walker, freezing with panic. "Where are they?"

"Down here," yelled Lone wolf, already at the river's edge thirty yards down.

Two Owls popped out of the water with the doe in his arms. He wobbled once, the deer kicked, and they fell once again into the raging fury.

"Help them!" Morning Star ran from the fire, dropping her cup of coffee as she ran.

Two Owls emerged again, fifty yards later, with the deer still in his arms. Finding his footing near the bank, he stood and emerged from the water with the young, lifeless doe in his grasp. He coughed a few times, then set the doe gently on the ground.

"Are you alright?" Questioned Morning Star as she wrapped her arms around her drenched husband. "You could have been killed."

"I'm okay," he answered, returning her

embrace. "One of you boys bring me my jacket."

Badger ran back to the lodge and retrieved a wool jacket. "Here it is," he held the jacket at arms length, and grinned.

A small crowd gathered to watch Two Owls dry the fallen doe. Her eyes, wide and brown, stared up at the man kneeling at her side. She coughed, and shivered as the wool jacket was placed across her body.

"Back up everyone," said Two Owls, standing to his feet with Morning Star still at his side. "Let her catch her breath and warm up. I think she will be fine."

The crowd scattered, and the rest of them followed Two Owls back to the fire pit for a lengthy game of questions, and answers.

"Don't ever do that again," said Running Moon, fighting back the urge to cry. "You could have died."

"That innocent deer could have died too if I didn't help."

The group sat in near silence, pondering the

events of the morning, as we watched the young doe. She stood to her feet, letting the wool slide from her back, looked back at her shaking legs, and took a single step toward us.

Her head raised until she made eye contact with the man who pulled her from death's hands, and if looks could speak, she said, thank you brother. Thank you for saving my life. She then climbed the side of the mountain, and vanished beneath the warm springtime sun.

ACTS OF INSANITY

When you have everything to lose,
and nothing real to gain,
yet you do those things you know are right,
you might be labeled as insane.

Insanity to some they say
is based on how one feels,
and to always give to those in need
gives strength that always heals.

Stay true to that that keeps you whole,
and do those things you do.
To hell with what the others think,
your insanity may save you.

SKUNK BRITCHES

Food Tent Terror

Six days have already passed on this ten day excursion into the untamed wilderness. It is said that with a sharp knife, knowledge of direction, and a touch of common sense, a man can easily survive ten simple days in the unknown. That is, unless, something turns the expected into an unexpected disaster.

Evening came quietly in the valley of the setting sun, and unseen to an adventurous four, nightfall set the scene for an unwelcome nightmare. A terror so horrifying, that even the passage of time could not mend the dreadful damage.

Raven, the dark haired, most aggressive of the group, sat next to a roaring fire as he skinned a common field mouse with surgical precision. With nothing more than a wooden stump for a table, and a small lock blade pocket knife, he completed his work with detailed accuracy.

"Look," he said with his devilish grin of accomplishment. "This thing still has it's eyelids." He held the tiny hide between his fingers.

"Has anyone ever told you that you're a sick man?" Asked Chris, studying the miniature remains.

"All the time," answered Raven, stretching the mouse hide across the stump. "Do we have any spare salt?"

"Yes, it's in the food cooler in the tent," answered Spirit Walker as he placed a couple logs across the fire. "I'm going over there so I can bring it back. Does anyone else need anything?"

"No thanks," they each said in their own unique ways as they began to clean up camp for the night.

Spirit Walker flipped the switch on his flashlight

and aimed the beam toward the nylon storage tent. He held the light in his teeth, unzipped the mesh door, and began rummaging for the salt.

Pans rattled, and cans rolled around as he retrieved the salt and cleaned up the mess. Once things were put away, and the lids were all closed on the coolers, he crawled out and zipped the tent closed.

"Here's the salt," he said, passing the container to Raven. "You can use the rest of it. We have another can in the food tent."

"Thanks."

"What are you going to do with that thing?"

"I don't know," answered Raven as he poured salt on the hide. "Maybe I can turn it into a medicine bag, or something." He emptied the salt container and tossed the cardboard into the fire.

"I'm going to call it a day."

"I'll be in as soon as this fire dies down," replied Raven, moving the coals around with a stick.

"See you in the morning than," Spirit Walker

walked over to the tent to join Skunk Britches, and Chris, who were already sound asleep.

"Good night brother," said Raven as he stared into the glowing embers.

"Good night."

The sounds of darkness changed the gentle flow of the river into mischievous whispers of unrecognizable children, and the scurrying of tiny claws on canvas could have been nothing less than the sounds of tearing flesh. Still of night carries a strange sort of silence, but this night was only still for a few hours.

Crash... Rattle, rattle.

"What the hell was that?" Raven was the first to jump out of bed as he yelled.

"I don't know," answered Chris, feeling his heart pounding in his chest.

Squeal, hiss... Hiss, rattle.

"It sounds like it's in the food tent," whispered Skunk Britches as he reached for his flashlight, and his knife.

"It sounds like several things are fighting in there, but I zipped it closed." Spirit walker pulled his knife from it's sheath, and held it tight.

The sound of pots, and pans smashing together grew louder, and the squeals continued for, in the dark of night, seems, an eternity.

"What do you think it is?" Asked Chris as he and Skunk Britches turned on their flashlights.

"I don't know," replied Raven, sliding his second boot on. "I'm going to club it though." He untied the tent door ans slid quietly through the narrow opening.

Silence...

"Ahhh!" Ravens scream echoed through the canyon, and the squeals grew faint and vanished into the darkness.

Two angry eyes peered through the opening of the tent just before Raven stumbled in. "I am Screams at Skunks. Defender of food," A wooden club fell from his hand, and he sat at the foot of his bed.
"Did you hear them scream as they ran away?"

"Were they in the food tent?" Asked Spirit Walker, placing his knife back in it's sheath.

"Yes, that's where they came running from."

"Crap," Chris plugged his nose. "I can smell them."

"How did they get in the food tent?" Asked Skunk Britches as he too plugged his nose.

"I think they pushed the zipper up. Do you want to know the worse part about them getting in there?" A large grin crawled upon Raven's face.

"What?"

"They were in there when they sprayed."

"Well," said Spirit Walker as he laid his head on his pillow. "I am glad that the food is still in the coolers. We can check out the damage in the morning."

"I can't sleep now. Chasing them skunks woke me up. Besides, it's getting light out there, and it smells bad in here."

"You go build a fire," said Spirit Walker. "I will check on the food tent, and get some coffee going."

"I'll be up in a few hours," said Skunk Britches, pulling his sleeping bag over his head. "I'm not ready to get up."

Chris finished untying the tent door and stepped outside with Raven while Spirit Walker finished getting dressed. The distinct, ammonia based, scent of skunk was heavy in the cool morning air, and the closer they got to the food tent, the more it burned their eyes.

Chris unzipped the tent and let the fabric fall to the side as he stumbled backward. "I can't breathe."

Spirit Walker took a step back and crouched to look inside. Scattered flower looked like snow on the bottom of the tent, and pieces of bread had been tossed into each area not already occupied by chunks of wiener, jerky, or assorted fruit.

"I can't believe that those skunks unzipped our tent, and opened the coolers." He took a deep breath and leaned in to grab the can of coffee. "Raven!"

"What?" Raven placed another piece of kindling on the fire before walking to the nylon tent.

"There's shit in here," said Spirit Walker,

handing Raven the coffee and a bag of sugar. He moved away from the tent and stood to breathe the less than fresh air. "Look in there."

Raven crouched to look in the tent and grinned. "That's great," he said, standing up again. "I scared the crap out of them when I screamed."

"Yes you did, and I think that you should be the one to clean it up." Spirit walker took the coffee from Raven, filled a pot with water, and placed the fixings on the fire to brew.

"I think we should get all of the food out of there, and drop the whole tent into the river," said Chris as he set a chair by the fire, and sat. "You should just throw it away."

"I'll see if the river will rinse it first," replied Spirit Walker, walking back to the food tent to retrieve a box of toaster pastries. "Anyone want breakfast, they smell like skunk."

"I'll eat one," said Raven. "I'm hungry."

"You're always hungry." Spirit walker held the box at arms length. "Get this box away from me before I throw up."

"Let me have one," said Chris as he stood to take the box from Raven.

"Save one for me." Skunk Britches stepped out of the tent and opened a Mountain Choice soda.

Raven was the first to open the individual package and take a bite. "Oh crap!" The pastry fell from his mouth as he turned his head to spit. "They taste like shit."

Chris, and Skunk Britches spit their breakfast into the fire, and Chris wiped his tongue with the sleeve of his shirt to remove the small crumbs. "Pour me some coffee so I can get this taste out of my mouth."

"It tastes like skunk," said Skunk Britches as he
 chugged his soda.

Spirit walker poured three cups of coffee, and mixed cold water with them to cool them down. He passed the others their cups, and stirred a spoon of sugar into his own.

Chris quickly took a sip and spit it out. "This tasted bad too. I bet everything in that tent is ruined now."

Raven took a second sip of his coffee. He moved it from cheek to cheek, then swallowed. "It's not as bad as the pastry," he said with a grimace
 before taking another sip. "We have four
 days left on our trip, so I think I can get used to it."

"There are two options," said Skunk Britches, opening another soda. "We can eat skunk for a few days, or we can go home and call ourselves weak."

"I'm staying," replied Raven, chugging the rest of the coffee in his cup.

"Me too," said Chris and Spirit Walker at the same time.

Skunk Britches pulled a chair around to the fire and sat next to Chris. "It looks like we will all eat skunk flavored food. I'm staying too, and from now on, we will call Raven, Screams at skunks,"

SPIRIT WALKER CHRIS CERESOLA RAVEN

Watch for more true tales of the Four Winds in volume 02, and be sure to check out more literature by, David James Hooton online at www.davidhooton.net

Check out our talented friends at

www.kevinkula.net

www.ingramcontent.com/pod-product-compliance
Lightning Source LLC
Chambersburg PA
CBHW070526290526
45790CB00003B/1321